My World of Science

USING ELECTRICITY

Angela Royston

Heinemann Library
Chicago, Illinois

Designed by bigtop
Originated by Ambassador Litho
Printed and bound in Hong Kong/China

06 05 04 03 02
10 9 8 7 6 5 4 3 2 1

Library of Congress Cataloging-in-Publication Data
Royston, Angela.
  Using electricity.
    p. cm. -- (My world of science)
Includes bibliographical references and index.
  ISBN 1-58810-239-4 (lib. bdg.)   ISBN 1-4034-0046-6 (pbk. bdg.)
  1. Electricity--Juvenile literature. [1. Electricity.] I. Title.
  QC527.2 .R69 2001
  537--dc21
                              00-012876

Acknowledgments
The author and publishers are grateful to the following for permission to reproduce copyright material:

Trevor Clifford, pp. 6, 7, 9, 10, 11, 12, 13, 14, 15, 16, 17, 18, 19, 20, 21, 22, 23, 24, 26, 27, 28, 29; Corbis, pp. 5, 8, 25; H. Rogers/Trip, p. 4.

Cover photograph reproduced with permission of Corbis.

Every effort has been made to contact copyright holders of any material reproduced in this book. Any omissions will be rectified in subsequent printings if notice is given to the publisher.

Some words are shown in bold, **like this.** You can find out what they mean by looking in the glossary.

Contents

What Is Electricity?

Electrical **power** is a kind of energy that can be changed into other kinds of energy, such as heat, light, and motion.

Electricity is used in **machines** in schools, stores, offices, and even in the street. Electricity makes the signs on these buildings light up.

Using Electricity

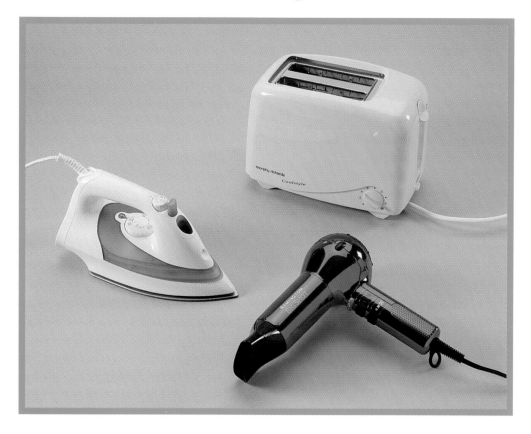

Electrical **power** can be changed into heat, sound, or movement as well as into light. These **machines** all use electricity to make heat.

A television uses electricity to make light, pictures, and sounds. A vacuum cleaner uses electricity to suck up dust. It also makes a lot of noise.

Where Does Electricity Come From?

Electricity is made in **power stations.** It is sent along wires to houses, stores, and other buildings. The electrical wires are joined to **sockets** in the walls.

When an electric plug is pushed into
a socket, electricity **flows** into the
machine. Some sockets have **switches**
that stop the electricity from flowing.

Danger!

Be careful—electricity can be dangerous. An electric **shock** may hurt or kill you. Never poke things into **sockets** or electrical **machines.**

Once an electric iron, toaster, or oven is hot, it can take a long time to cool down. Be careful not to touch these things after they have been used.

What Is a Battery?

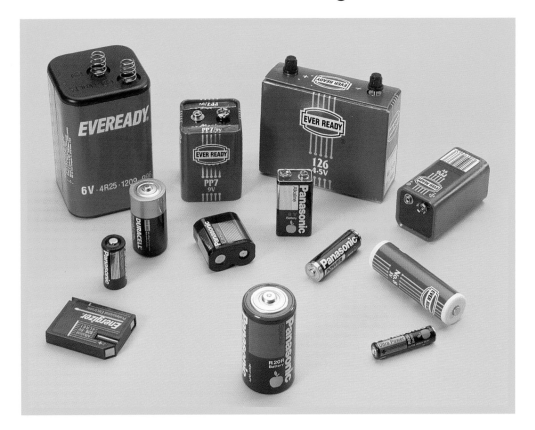

A battery stores electricity. **Chemicals** inside the battery slowly change to make electricity. Batteries are made in different shapes and sizes.

The batteries in this **remote control** make only a small amount of electricity. They make enough electricity to make the remote control work, but not enough to make it hot.

Machines that Use Batteries

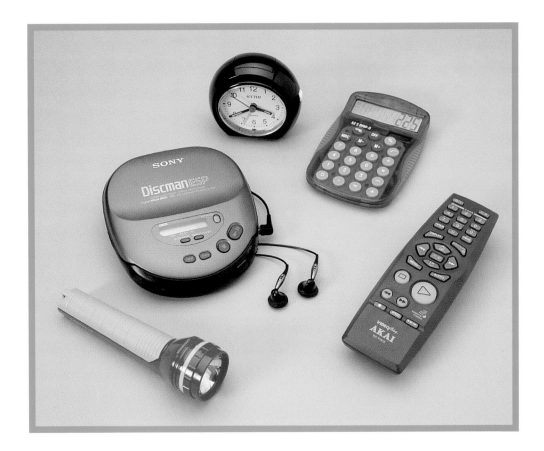

Batteries are useful because you can carry them around. All of these **machines** use batteries so that you can take them with you.

Batteries do not last forever. After
a while they cannot make electricity.
When the batteries in these toys are
used up, the toys will stop working.

Taking a Flashlight Apart

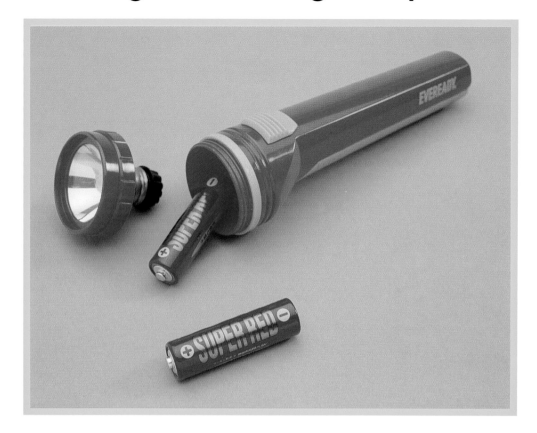

Look at one of the batteries inside a flashlight. One end is flat and has a "−" sign on the side. The other end has a bump with a "+" sign.

Each battery has to be loaded the right way in order to make the flashlight work. The "+" end of the battery must touch the "−" sign in the flashlight.

What Is a Circuit?

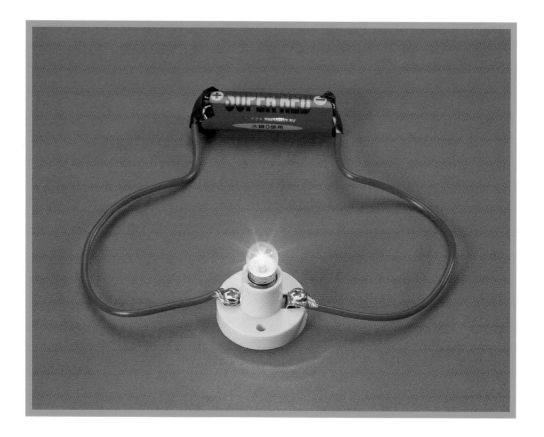

A **circuit** is a pathway for electricity to **flow** along. Electricity flows from the battery through the wire, through the lightbulb, and back to the battery.

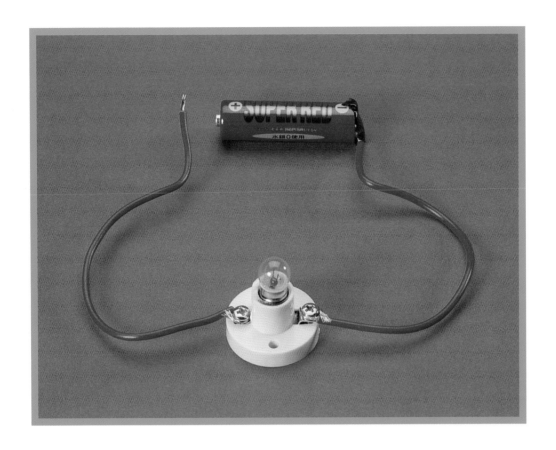

Electricity will flow only if the pathway makes a complete loop. Here the loop has been broken. The electricity stops flowing and the light goes out.

Lighting Two Bulbs

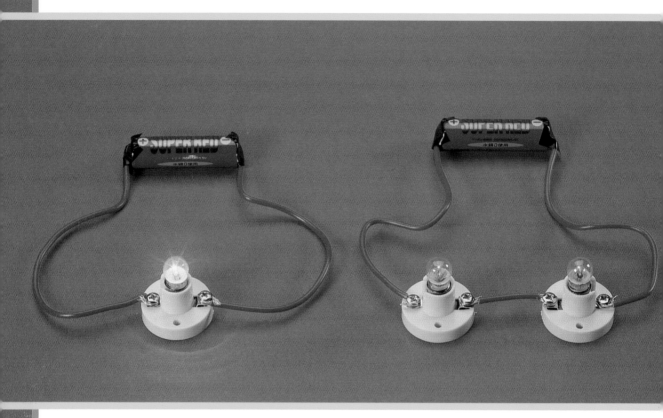

You can add one or more lightbulbs
to a **circuit.** Every time you add one,
the light each lightbulb makes will
be dimmer.

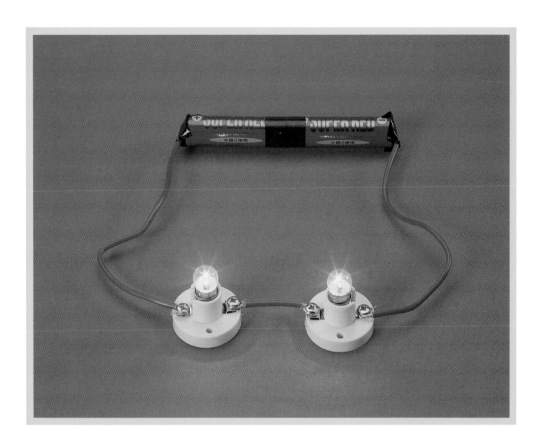

A battery can only make a fixed amount of electricity. If you add another battery, it adds more electricity. Here, the lightbulbs are shining brightly.

Switches

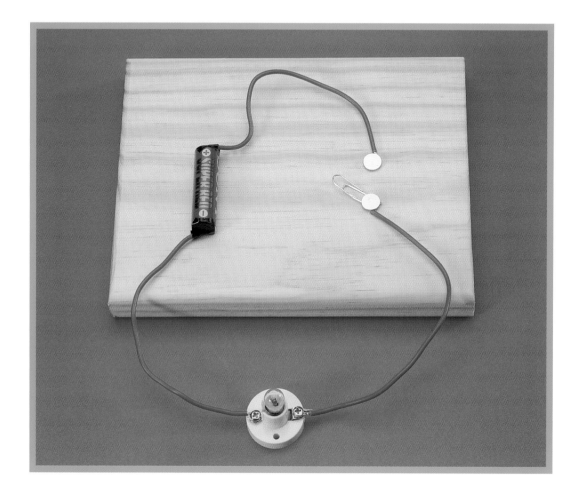

A **switch** allows you to break a **circuit.**
The paper clip is the switch in this circuit.
When the switch is off, electricity cannot
flow around the circuit.

This switch controls an electric train circuit. When the switch is on, the train moves around the track. What will happen when the switch is turned off?

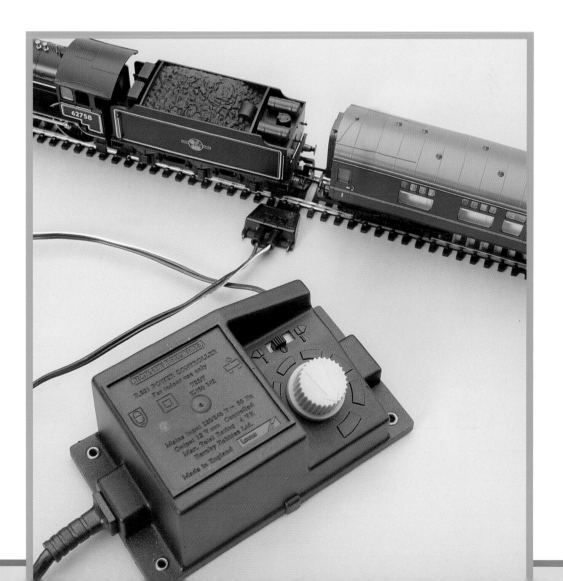

Conductors

A **conductor** is something that lets electricity **flow** through it easily. This girl is testing metal foil to see whether electricity will flow through it.

The electricity flows through the metal foil. Metal is a good conductor. It is used for the wires that carry electricity for electric trains.

Insulators

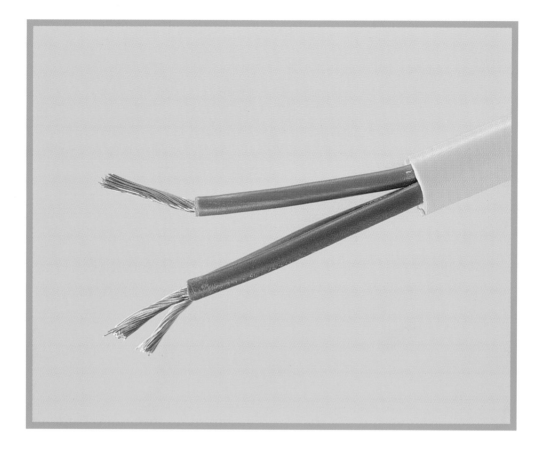

An **insulator** is something that electricity cannot **flow** through. Plastic is a good insulator. That is why electrical wires are usually covered with plastic.

This girl is testing things to see whether they are insulators or **conductors.** When she tests an insulator, the electricity stops flowing.

Drawing a Circuit

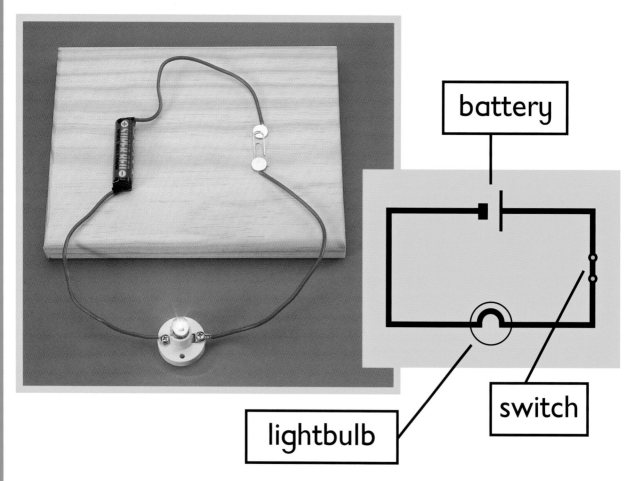

battery

lightbulb

switch

You can draw a **circuit** using simple symbols for the battery, **switch,** wire, and lightbulb. Is the switch in this circuit open or closed?

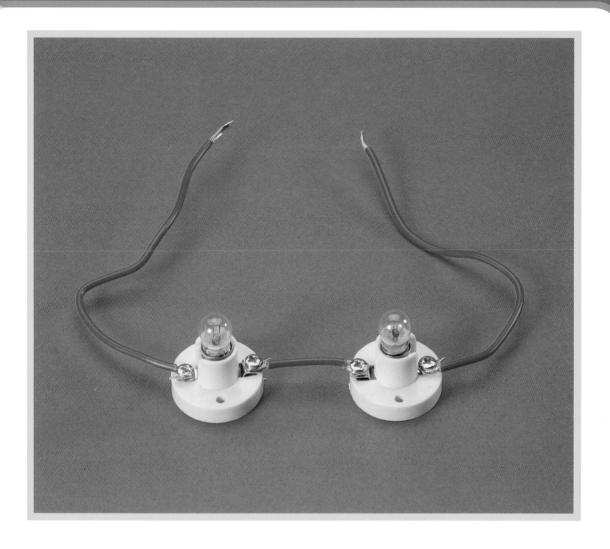

There is something wrong with this circuit. Someone has forgotten the battery. Make a drawing to show what the circuit should look like.

Glossary

chemical type of substance

circuit pathway for electricity to flow along

conductor something that electricity can move smoothly through

flow to move smoothly

force something that makes things move

insulator something that blocks electricity

machine something that uses force to get something done

power strength or energy

power station building where electricity is made

remote control something that allows you to turn a machine off and on from a distance

shock burning from electricity going through your body

socket holes an electric plug is fitted into, usually found on the wall

switch something that opens or closes an electric circuit

More Books to Read

Evans, Nevile. *The Science of a Lightbulb.* Austin, Tex.: Raintree Steck-Vaughn. An older reader can help you with this book.

Parker, Steve. *Electricity and Magnetism.* Austin, Tex.: Raintree Steck-Vaughn Publishers, 2000.

Index